Introduction

This book supports students preparing for the Edexcel GCSE exam. The pr: the book are carefully modelled after past papers and specifications of ⟨ ensure that the papers as a whole provide a rich and varied practice to meet all requirements of GCSE mathematics with an appropriate difficulty.

Papers are designed to teach students the most easily applicable, reusable and fastest solutions to typical problems, and utilise problems which target areas of maths which students typically forget under the pressure of an exam. Solutions provided have been reviewed by many students to ensure that they are easily understandable while being the fastest and most re-applicable.

The practice papers cover the following six distinct topic areas:
1. Fundamental Number Operations
2. Algebra
3. Ratio, proportion, and rates of change
4. Geometry and measures
5. Probability
6. Statistics

After completing these practice papers, you should be able to:
1. Quickly formulate optimal solutions to any GCSE mathematics question.
2. More readily apply previously learnt skills on a question to question basis.

GCSE Mathematics Practice Papers comprises of 2 books, calculator and non-calculator. Each book contains 4 full practice papers, while each practice paper contains 20 questions and solutions.

Contents

Paper 1 (Non-Calculator)

Materials
For this paper you must have:
- Ruler graduated in centimetres and millimetres, protractor, compasses, pen, HB pencil, eraser.
- Tracing paper may be used.

Time allowed
1 hour 30 minutes.

Instructions
- Use black ink or black ball-point pen. Draw diagrams in pencil.
- Answer all questions.
- You must answer the questions in the space provided.
- You must show all your working.
- Diagrams are not accurately drawn, unless otherwise indicated.
- Calculators may not be used.

Information
- The marks for questions are shown in brackets.
- The maximum mark is 80.

Advice
- Read each question carefully before you start to answer it.
- Keep an eye on the time.
- Try to answer every question.
- Check your answers if you have time at the end.

1

1   The diagram shows a square with side 4 cm. Points *A*, *B*, *C* and *D* are quarter of the ways along the sides.

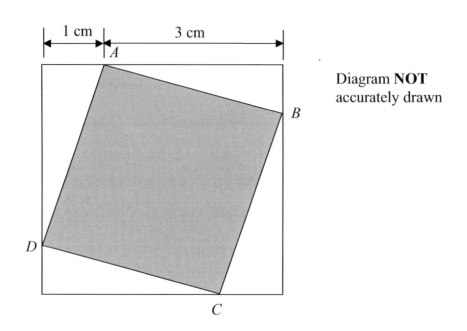

Diagram **NOT** accurately drawn

Work out the proportion of the area inside the square that is shaded.

....

....

....

....

....

....

....

....

....

....

....

....

....

....

....

Answer...................................   (4 marks)   4

2   Triangle *ABC* has perimeter 15 cm

$AB = 5$ cm, $BC = 4$ cm.

Show that *ABC* is an acute triangle.

……………………………………………………………………………..................

……………………………………………………………………………..................

……………………………………………………………………………..................

……………………………………………………………………………..................

……………………………………………………………………………..................

(4 marks)

3   The diagram shows a solid prism with the same cross-section through its length.
The cross-section is a trapezium with height 40 cm. The top *EFGH* is a rectangle of
width 20 cm and length 30 cm, the base *ABCD* is rectangle of width 20 cm and
length 40 cm. The prism is made from wood with density 0.0005 kg/cm³.
Work out the mass of the prism.

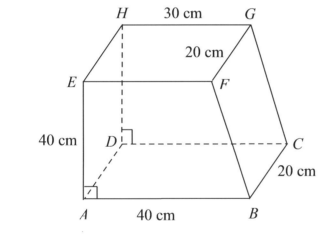

……………………………………………………………………………..................

……………………………………………………………………………..................

……………………………………………………………………………..................

……………………………………………………………………………..................

……………………………………………………………………………..................

……………………………………………………………………………..................

……………………………………………………………………………..................

……………………………………………………………………………..................

Answer…………………………….   (4 marks)

4   Here are a trapezium and a right-angled triangle. The area of the triangle is the same as the area of the trapezium.

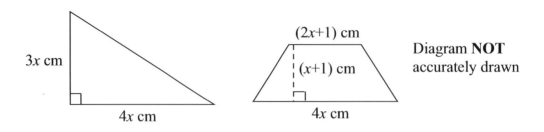

$3x$ cm

$4x$ cm

$(2x+1)$ cm

$(x+1)$ cm

$4x$ cm

Diagram **NOT** accurately drawn

Show that $6x^2 - 7x = 1$

....

....

....

....

(4 marks)

5   *BA* is a diameter of this circle and is extended to point *S*. *ST* is a tangent meeting the circle at point *T*. *O* is the centre of the circle. *AT=AO*

Prove that triangle *ATB* is congruent to triangle *OTS*.

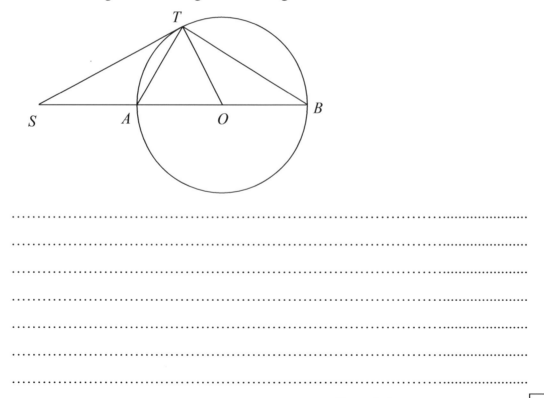

....

....

....

....

....

....

....

(4 marks)

8

4

6   Triangle **A** and triangle **B** are similar.

Triangle **A** has a circumference of 150 cm

Triangle **B** has a circumference of 30 cm

Triangle **A** has an area of 1000 cm²

Calculate the area of triangle **B**.

....

....

....

....

....

....

Answer............................   (3 marks)

7   Emma has a biased coin. When the coin is thrown once, the probability that the coin will land heads is 0.4. Emma throws the coin twice.

7(a)   Complete and fully label the probability tree diagram to show the possible outcome.

1st   2nd

0.4   heads

tails

(4 marks)

7(b)   Calculate the probability that the coin will land heads at least once.

....

....

....

Answer............................   (2 marks)

9

5

8   There are 20 boys and 10 girls in a class. They took maths challenge. The mean mark for boys is 55%, the mean mark for the class is 50%.

Work out the mean mark for the girls.

....

....

....

....

....

....

Answer............................   (2 marks)

9   The table shows information about the height of some plants.

Height (cm)	$0 < h \leq 20$	$20 < h \leq 30$	$30 < h \leq 40$	$40 < h \leq 70$
Number of plants	24	38	33	30

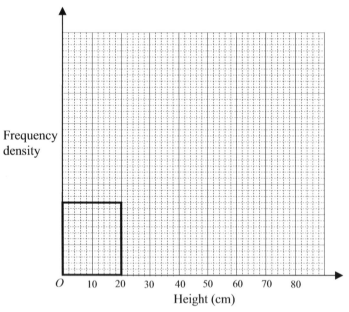

9(a)   Complete the histogram for this information.

....

....

....

....

(4 marks)

6

6

9(b) Work out an estimate for the number of plants which the height is greater more than 52 cm

....

....

....

....

Answer……………………………   (3 marks)

10 The first four terms of an arithmetic sequence are

2   6   10   14

Work out an expression, in terms of n, for the nth term.

....

....

....

....

Answer……………………………   (3 marks)

11(a) Simplify $(p^2 \times p^3)^2$

....

....

....

....

....

Answer……………………………   (2 marks)

11(b) Simplify fully $\dfrac{3x}{(x-2)(x-4)} + \dfrac{3}{x-2}$

....

....

....

....

....

....

Answer……………………………   (2 marks)

10

11(c) Factorise $8x^2 - 18$

....

....

....

....

Answer................................   (2 marks)

12(a) Express $2^{100} + 2^{102}$ in the form $m \times 2^{100}$, m is an integer.

....

....

....

....

Answer................................   (2 marks)

12(b) Express $2^{100} + 2^{102}$ in the form $n \times 4^{50}$, n is an integer.

....

....

....

....

Answer................................   (2 marks)

13(a) Write 1.5×10^{-4} as an ordinary number.

....

....

....

Answer................................   (2 marks)

13(b) Work out the value of $4.8 \times 10^5 \div (4 \times 10^{-6})$

Give your answer in standard form.

....

....

....

Answer................................   (2 marks)

$\boxed{10}$

14   On 1 April 2019, the cost of 5 grams of gold was £220. The cost of gold increased by 10% from 1 April 2018 to 1 April 2019.

Work out the cost of 20 grams of gold on 1 April 2018.

....

....

....

....

....

....

....

Answer…………………………….   (3 marks)

15   P is directly proportional to Q^2 where $Q > 0$. $P = 400$ when $Q = 10$.

15(a)   Find a formula for P in terms of Q.

....

....

....

....

....

....

Answer…………………………….   (3 marks)

15(b)   Find the value of Q when $P = 36$.

....

....

....

....

Answer…………………………….   (2 marks)

8

16 *a, b, c* and d are consecutive integers.

Explain why $ab + cd$ is always even.

....

....

....

....

....

....

....

....

(3 marks)

17 Solve the simultaneous equations

$2x + y = 13$

$x + y = 8$

....

....

....

....

....

....

....

....

....

....

....

....

....

Answer................................   (2 marks)

5

18   The diagram shows part of the graph of $y = f(x)$

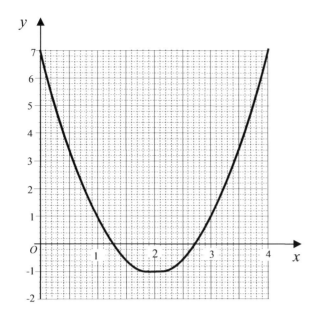

18(a) Find $f(3)$

……………………………………………………………………………………............……

……………………………………………………………………………………............……

……………………………………………………………………………………............……

        Answer……………………………….   (2 marks)

18(b) Write down the coordinates of the turning point of the graph

……………………………………………………………………………….....................……

……………………………………………………………………………….....................……

……………………………………………………………………………….....................……

……………………………………………………………………………….....................……

        Answer……………………………….   (2 marks)

18(c) Write down estimates for the roots of $f(x) = 0$.

       Give your answers to 1 decimal place.

……………………………………………………………………………….....................……

……………………………………………………………………………….....................……

……………………………………………………………………………….....................……

……………………………………………………………………………….....................……

        Answer……………………………….   (2 marks)

6

19 The equation of line L_1 is $y = 2x - 3$

The equation of line L_2 is $2y + x = 10$

Show that these two lines are perpendicular.

………………………………………………………………………........................

………………………………………………………………………........................

………………………………………………………………………........................

………………………………………………………………………........................

………………………………………………………………………........................

………………………………………………………………………........................

………………………………………………………………………........................

………………………………………………………………………........................

………………………………………………………………………........................

………………………………………………………………………........................

(3 marks)

20 $OABC$ is a parallelogram. M is the midpoint of OC.

$\overrightarrow{OA} = \mathbf{x}$, $\overrightarrow{AB} = \mathbf{y}$.

Work out the vector of $\overrightarrow{AM}$

Give your answer in terms of $\mathbf{x}$ and $\mathbf{y}$.

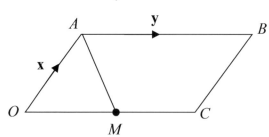

………………………………………………………………………........................

………………………………………………………………………........................

………………………………………………………………………........................

………………………………………………………………………........................

Answer……………………………….   (3 marks)

Paper 2 (Non-Calculator)

Materials
For this paper you must have:
- Ruler graduated in centimetres and millimetres, protractor, compasses, pen, HB pencil, eraser.
- Tracing paper may be used.

Time allowed
1 hour 30 minutes.

Instructions
- Use black ink or black ball-point pen. Draw diagrams in pencil.
- Answer all questions.
- You must answer the questions in the space provided.
- You must show all your working.
- Diagrams are not accurately drawn, unless otherwise indicated.
- Calculators may not be used.

Information
- The marks for questions are shown in brackets.
- The maximum mark is 80.

Advice
- Read each question carefully before you start to answer it.
- Keep an eye on the time.
- Try to answer every question.
- Check your answers if you have time at the end.

1(a)   Expand and simplify $(3+2\sqrt{3})(2+3\sqrt{3})$

Give your answer in the form $a+b\sqrt{3}$, where a and b are integers.

Show your working clearly.

....

....

....

....

   Answer............................... (2 marks)

1(b)   Factorise $16x^2-9$

....

....

....

....

   Answer............................... (2 marks)

1(c)   Simplify the expression $(2x^3y^2)^3$

....

....

....

....

   Answer............................... (2 marks)

2   Solve the equation $x^2-4x-2=0$

Give your answer in the form $a\pm\sqrt{b}$, where a and b are integers.

....

....

....

....

   Answer............................... (2 marks)

8

3   Rationalise the denominator and simply fully $\dfrac{6}{\sqrt{3}-3}$

....

....

....

....

Answer……………………………   (2 marks)

4   Work out the range of values of x for which $x^2-3x-10<0$

....

....

....

....

Answer……………………………   (2 marks)

5   Find an approximate value for $\dfrac{4.125\times10^6}{7.997\times10^{-4}}$

Give your answer in standard form.

....

....

....

....

Answer……………………………   (3 marks)

6   A bag contains red and blue beads. The ratio of red beads to blue beads is 3:2.

The number of red beads is decreased by 20%.

The number of blue beads is increased by 40%

There are now 52 beads in total in the bag.

Work out how many blue beads were originally.

....

....

....

....

Answer……………………………   (3 marks)

10

7   A line passes through $(4,3)$ with gradient 2.

Work out the equation of the line and write down the equation in the form $y = mx + c$

……………………………………………………………………………………....................

……………………………………………………………………………………....................

……………………………………………………………………………………....................

……………………………………………………………………………………....................

Answer……………………………   (2 marks)

8    $(m + p)x + (m - p) \equiv 4x + 6$, where m and p are integers.

Work out the values of m and p.

……………………………………………………………………………………....................

……………………………………………………………………………………....................

……………………………………………………………………………………....................

……………………………………………………………………………………....................

Answer……………………………   (2 marks)

9   You are given that $5.6 \times 13.2 = 73.92$ exactly.

9(a)   Emma says that $56 \times 0.0132 = 7.392$

Without doing an exact calculation, show that Emma is wrong.

……………………………………………………………………………………....................

……………………………………………………………………………………....................

……………………………………………………………………………………....................

……………………………………………………………………………………....................

(3 marks)

9(b)   Find the exact value of 0.056×132

……………………………………………………………………………………....................

……………………………………………………………………………………....................

……………………………………………………………………………………....................

……………………………………………………………………………………....................

Answer……………………………   (3 marks)

10

16

10   P is inversely proportional to Q^2 where $Q > 0$. $P = 100$ when $Q = 6$.

Find the value of Q when $P = 36$.

……………………………………………………………………………...................

……………………………………………………………………………...................

……………………………………………………………………………...................

……………………………………………………………………………...................

      Answer…………………………….   (3 marks)

11     $PQRS$ is a trapezium, as shown in the diagram. $\angle SPQ = 60^0$. RQ is perpendicular to

SR and PQ.

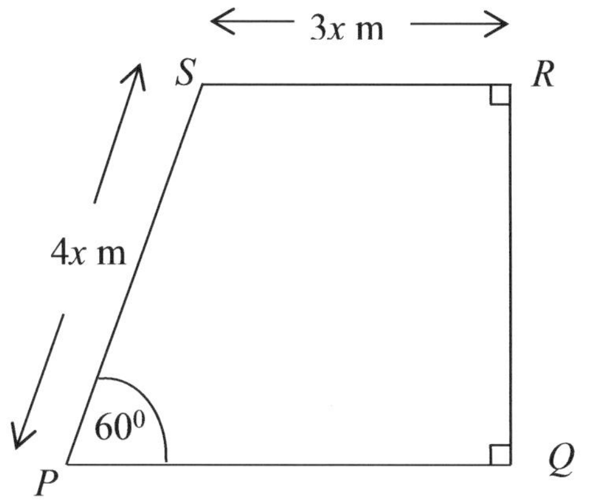

Diagram **NOT** accurately drawn

Work out the area of the trapezium, in terms of x

………………………………………………………………………………………...................

………………………………………………………………………………………...................

………………………………………………………………………………………...................

………………………………………………………………………………………...................

………………………………………………………………………………………...................

………………………………………………………………………………………...................

………………………………………………………………………………………...................

      Answer…………………………….   (3 marks)

6

17

12   Here is a triangle. $\sin x^0 = \dfrac{3\sqrt{3}}{8}$

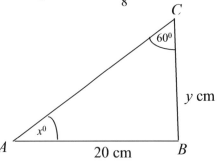

Diagram **NOT**
accurately drawn

Work out the value of y.

....

....

....

....

        Answer.............................   (3 marks)

13   A, B, C and D are on the circumference of a circle, DT is a tangent to the circle at
      D.

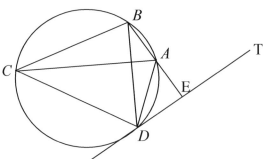

Prove that triangle ADE is similar to triangle DBE.

....

....

....

....

....

                                              (3 marks)

6

14   *OABC* is a parallelogram. *M* is the midpoint of *OC*.

$\overrightarrow{OA} = \mathbf{x}$, $\overrightarrow{AB} = \mathbf{y}$.

Show by a vector method that *AM* is parallel to *OD*

....

....

....

....

....

....

....

....

....

....

....

....

....

....

....

....

....

....

(3 marks)

3

15(a) Shape **P** is reflected in the *x*-axis to give shape **Q**.

Shape **Q** is reflected in the line *x* = -1 to give shape **R**.

Describe fully the single transformation that maps shape **P** onto shape **R**

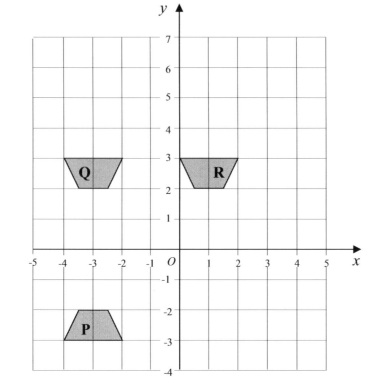

....

....

....

Answer……………………………….   (3 marks)

15(b) On the grid, enlarge shape **R** with scale factor 2 and centre *O*, and label it **S** on the grid.

....

....

....

....

....

(3 marks)

16   A box contains toy cars. Each car is red or black or blue.

Jack takes a car at random from the box.

The table shows the probabilities that Jack takes a red car or a blue car.

Colour of car	Probability
red	0.50
blue	0.30
black	

16(a) Work out the probability that Jack takes a black car.

....

....

....

....

....

Answer…………………………….   (2 marks)

16(b) Jack adds 50 black cars into the box. The following table shows the probabilities that Jack takes a red car or a blue car or a black car or silver after he adds 50 black cars into the box.

Colour of car	Probability
red	0.40
blue	0.24
black	0.36

Work out the total number of cars in the box originally.

....

....

....

....

....

....

Answer…………………………….   (4 marks)

6

17   The scatter graph shows the heights of boys at different ages.

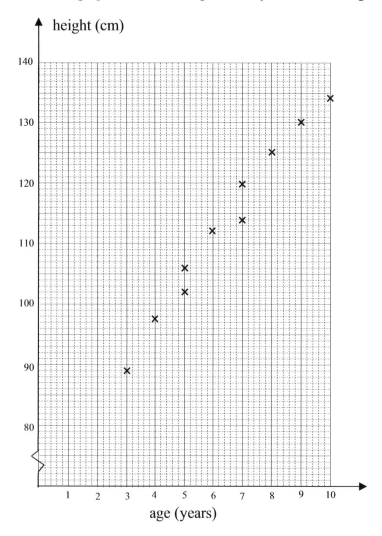

17(a) Draw a line of best fit on the scatter graph.

....

....

....

....

(4 marks)

17(b) Estimate the height of a one year old and comment on the reliability of your estimate.

....

....

....

(3 marks)

7

22

18   100 pupils took an examination paper. The table gives a summary of their results.

	Marks
Minimum	17
Lower quartile	46
Median	58
Upper quartile	72
Maximum	92

18(a) Draw a box plot to represent this information.

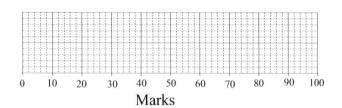

0   10   20   30   40   50   60   70   80   90   100

Marks

....

....

....

....

(3 marks)

18(b) Write down the interquartile range for these data.

....

....

....

....

Answer................................   (2 marks)

5

18(c) Work out an estimate for the number of these pupils with marks between 17 and 72.

....

....

....

....

Answer…………………………….   (2 marks)

18(d) Draw a cumulative frequency diagram to show the information.

....

....

....

....

(4 marks)

19   The diagram shows a circle, centre *C*. *TP* is a tangent to the circle and intersects the circle at *P*.

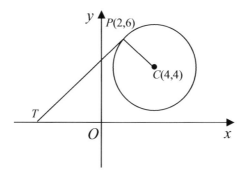

Work out the equation of line *TP*.

....

....

....

....

....

....

     Answer................................   (3 marks)

20   Here is the graph of $y = -2(x-2)^2 + 2$ for values of *x* from 0 to 4.

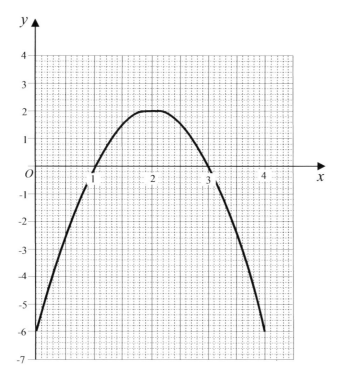

By drawing a suitable linear graph on the grid, work out approximate solutions of

$4x^2 - 19x + 20 = 0$.

Give your answers to 1 decimal place.

....

....

....

....

....

....

....

....

....

....

Answer................................ (4 marks)

Paper 3 (Non-Calculator)

Materials
For this paper you must have:
- Ruler graduated in centimetres and millimetres, protractor, compasses, pen, HB pencil, eraser.
- Tracing paper may be used.

Time allowed
1 hour 30 minutes.

Instructions
- Use black ink or black ball-point pen. Draw diagrams in pencil.
- Answer all questions.
- You must answer the questions in the space provided.
- You must show all your working.
- Diagrams are not accurately drawn, unless otherwise indicated.
- Calculators may not be used.

Information
- The marks for questions are shown in brackets.
- The maximum mark is 80.

Advice
- Read each question carefully before you start to answer it.
- Keep an eye on the time.
- Try to answer every question.
- Check your answers if you have time at the end.

1   Factorise fully $(x^2 - 16) + (x+4)(x+2)$

....

....

....

....

....

....

         Answer.................................   (2 marks)

2     $x^2 + px + q \equiv (x+2)^2 + 3$

    Work out the values of p and q.

....

....

....

....

         Answer.................................   (2 marks)

3   Simplify $(p^2 \times p^3)^2$

....

....

....

....

         Answer.................................   (2 marks)

4   Simplify fully $\dfrac{x+22}{(x-2)(x+4)} + \dfrac{3}{x+4}$

....

....

....

....

         Answer.................................   (2 marks)

8

5(a) Solve $(6-\sqrt{x})^{\frac{1}{2}}=2$

....

....

....

....

   Answer……………………….   (2 marks)

5(b) Solve $x^3-4x=0$

....

....

....

....

   Answer……………………….   (3 marks)

6     $x:y=5:3$ and $a:b=5x:3y$

   Work out $a:b$

   Give your answer in its simplest form.

....

....

....

....

   Answer……………………….   (2 marks)

7   Express 72 as the products of its prime factors.

....

....

....

....

   Answer……………………….   (2 marks)

9

8   Work out 104×96

....

....

....

....

Answer……………………………   (2 marks)

9(a)   Work out $4\frac{2}{7}+1\frac{2}{3}$

....

....

....

....

Answer……………………………   (3 marks)

9(b)   Work out $4\frac{2}{7}\div1\frac{2}{3}$

Give your answer as a mixed number in its simplest form.

....

....

....

....

Answer……………………………   (3 marks)

10   Expand and simplify $(x-1)(x-2)(x+2)$

....

....

....

....

Answer……………………………   (3 marks)

11   Emma buys a jumper.

20% VAT is added to the price of the jumper.

Emma has to pay a total of £60.

What is the price of the jumper with **no** VAT added?

…………………………………………………………………………..................……

…………………………………………………………………………..................……

…………………………………………………………………………..................……

…………………………………………………………………………..................……

Answer…………………………….   (3 marks)

12   In triangle ABC, $\cos B = \dfrac{1}{3}$

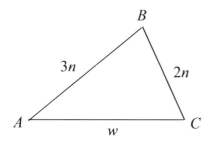

Show that triangle ABC is isosceles.

…………………………………………………………………………..................……

…………………………………………………………………………..................……

…………………………………………………………………………..................……

…………………………………………………………………………..................……

Answer…………………………….   (5 marks)

13   Here are a sphere and a cone. The base of the cone and the sphere have the same

radius r cm . l , the slant height, is $\sqrt{17}r$ cm.

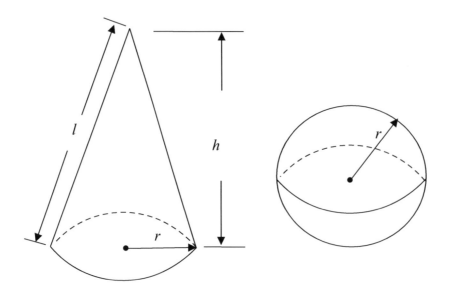

Prove that the sphere and the cone have the same volume.

....

....

....

....

....

....

....

....

....

....

....

....

(5 marks)

5

14   Point *P* and vectors **a** and **b** are shown on the grid.

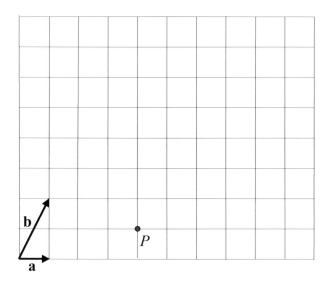

14(a) $\overrightarrow{PQ} = 2\mathbf{a} + 2\mathbf{b}$

On the grid, mark vector $\overrightarrow{PQ}$

....

....

....

....

....

....

....

(5 marks)

14(b) $\overrightarrow{PR} = -2\mathbf{a} + 2\mathbf{b}$

On the grid, mark vector $\overrightarrow{PR}$

....

....

....

....

....

....

....

(5 marks)

10

15   Find an equation of the line that is parallel to the line $y = 3x - 2$ and passes through the point (3,5).

....

....

....

....

Answer...................................   (3 marks)

16   The diagram shows the graph of $y = \sin x$ for $0^0 \leq x \leq 360^0$

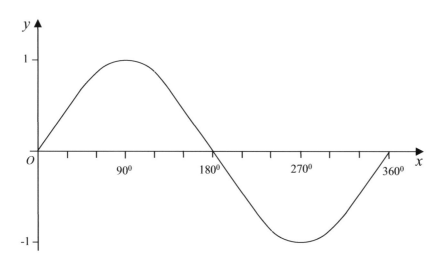

On the diagram above, sketch the graph of $y = \sin(x + 60^0)$ for $0^0 \leq x \leq 360^0$

....

....

....

....

....

....

....

(4 marks)

7

17   Here is the graph of $y = 2(x-2)^2 - 1$ for values of x from 0 to 4.

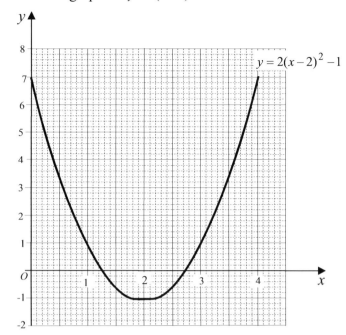

By drawing a suitable linear graph on the grid, work out approximate solutions of

$2x^2 - 9x + 6 = 0$.

Give your answers to 1 decimal place.

....

....

....

....

....

....

    Answer……………………………   (4 marks)

18   Mr Smith gives his class a test.

    10 girls in the class get a mean mark of 66%

    20 boys in the class get a mean mark of 72%

    Work out the mean mark for the whole class.

    ....

    ....

    ....

    ....

    Answer……………………………   (3 marks)

19   Emma keeps a record of the time that the school bus takes her from her home to school. Her record for last month is shown in the table.

Time, t minutes	Frequency
$10 < t \leq 12$	5
$12 < t \leq 14$	10
$14 < t \leq 16$	4
$16 < t \leq 18$	1

19(a)   There are 200 school days in the year.

Use the information in the table to estimate the number of days in a year on which Emma's bus journey takes more than 14 minutes. (Emma never misses a day of school.)

....

....

....

....

....

....

        Answer…………………………….   (4 marks)

19(b)   What is the probability that, on a randomly chosen day, the journey takes less than 12 minutes?

....

....

....

....

....

....

        Answer…………………………….   (4 marks)

8

20   A box contains toy cars. Each car is red or black or blue.

Jack takes a car at random from the box.

The table shows the probabilities that Jack takes a red car or a blue car.

Colour of car	Probability
red	0.50
blue	0.30
black	

20(a) Work out the probability that Jack takes a black car.

....

....

....

....

Answer……………………………….   (3 marks)

20(b) Jack puts the car back into the box. There are 4 black cars in the box.

Work out the number of red cars and the number of blue cars in the box.

Colour of car	The number of cars
red	
blue	

....

....

....

....

....

....

....

Answer………………………………   (4 marks)

7

37

Paper 4 (Non-Calculator)

Materials
For this paper you must have:
- Ruler graduated in centimetres and millimetres, protractor, compasses, pen, HB pencil, eraser.
- Tracing paper may be used.

Time allowed
1 hour 30 minutes.

Instructions
- Use black ink or black ball-point pen. Draw diagrams in pencil.
- Answer all questions.
- You must answer the questions in the space provided.
- You must show all your working.
- Diagrams are not accurately drawn, unless otherwise indicated.
- Calculators may not be used.

Information
- The marks for questions are shown in brackets.
- The maximum mark is 80.

Advice
- Read each question carefully before you start to answer it.
- Keep an eye on the time.
- Try to answer every question.
- Check your answers if you have time at the end.

1(a) a is a positive integer, show that $\sqrt{3a}(\sqrt{27a}+a\sqrt{3a})$ is always a multiple of 3.

....

....

....

....

(2 marks)

1(b) By factorising fully, simplify $\dfrac{x^4-3x^3+2x^2}{x^4-5x^2+4}$

....

....

....

....

(2 marks)

2 Rearrange $\dfrac{1}{x}+\dfrac{1}{y}=\dfrac{1}{w}$ to make y the subject.

$$\frac{1}{x}+\frac{1}{y}=\frac{1}{w} \Rightarrow \frac{1}{y}=\frac{x-w}{xw} \Rightarrow x=\frac{xw}{x-w}$$

Answer $y=\dfrac{xw}{x-w}$ (2 marks)

3(a) Find the lowest common multiple (LCM) of 8, 12 and 15

....

....

....

....

Answer   (3 marks)

3(b) Find the highest common factor (HCF) of 12, 18 and 36

....

....

....

Answer   (2 marks)

11

4(a) Solve $(2-\sqrt{x})^{\frac{1}{3}} = -1$

....

....

....

....

Answer…………………………..   (3 marks)

4(b) Solve $\sqrt{12} + \sqrt{48} = \sqrt{27} + \sqrt{x}$

....

....

....

....

Answer…………………………..   (3 marks)

4(c) Solve the simultaneous equations

$x^2 + y^2 = 10$ and $y = x + 4$

You must show your working.

....

....

....

....

Answer…………………………..   (2 marks)

5(a) Work out $3\frac{1}{3} \div 1\frac{3}{7}$

Give your answer as a mixed number in its simplest form.

....

....

....

....

Answer…………………………..   (3 marks)

5(b)   Rationalise the denominator and simply fully $\dfrac{\sqrt{2}-1}{2-\sqrt{2}}$

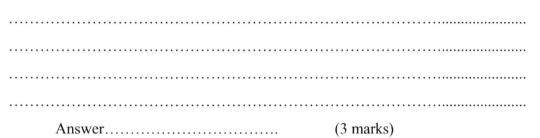

        Answer…………………………….   (3 marks)

6   Write $2x^2 - 12x + 5$ in the form $a(x+b)^2 + c$, where a, b and c are integers.

....

....

....

....

        Answer…………………………….   (3 marks)

7   Use ruler and compasses to construct the bisector of angle ABC.

        You must show all your construction lines.

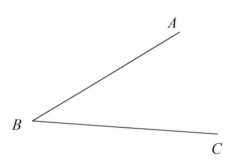

....

....

....

....

....

....

                                                (2 marks)

8

8   Find an approximate value for $8.96 \div 0.295$

You must show all your working.

....

....

....

....

Answer……………………………   (3 marks)

9   Write $0.3\dot{6}$ as a fraction in its simplest form.

....

....

....

....

Answer……………………………   (3 marks)

10   The lengths of the sides of a triangle are in the ratios 2 : 4 : 5. The length of the longest side of the triangle is 30 cm.

Work out the perimeter of the triangle.

....

....

....

....

Answer……………………………   (4 marks)

11   Jack buys 10 kg of sweets to sell. He pays £10 for the sweets. Jack puts all the sweets into bags. He puts 250 g of sweets into each bag. He sells each bag of sweets for 45p. Jack sells all the bags of sweets.

Work out his percentage profit.

....

....

....

....

Answer……………………………   (4 marks)

14

12   There are 6 blue marbles and 4 red marbles in a bag. Two marbles are taken at random from the bag.

Calculate, as an exactly fraction, the probability that both marbles are the same colour.

....

....

....

....

....

....

Answer................................   (4 marks)

13   Chocolate Bars are sold in two sizes.

A standard bar costs 50p and weighs 100 g. A king-size bar costs £1.00 and weighs 250 g.

Which size of bar is the better value for money?

....

....

....

....

....

Answer................................   (4 marks)

14   A company produces mugs in two sizes.

Small mugs are 6 cm high and can hold 100 cm^3 of liquid.

Large mugs are 12 cm high and are identical in shape to small mugs.

Work out the volume of a large mug.

....

....

....

....

....

Answer................................   (4 marks)   12

43

15   The diagram below shows a solid.

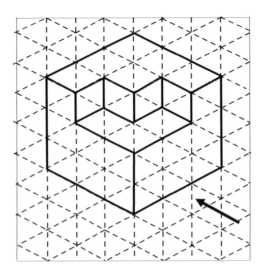

On the grid below, draw the elevation of this solid as seen from the direction of the

arrow.   (4 marks)

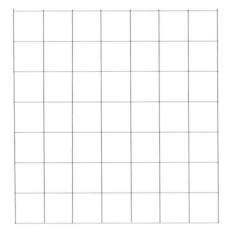

16   *ABC* and *DEA* are straight lines. *BE* is parallel to *CD*. $\angle DAC = 45^0$, $\angle ACD = 50^0$

Work out the size of $\angle AEB$.

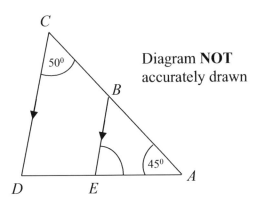

Diagram **NOT**
accurately drawn

....

....

....

....

....

....

        Answer................................   (4 marks)

17   A circle touches all vertices of the square. The radius of the circle is 10 cm as

shown.

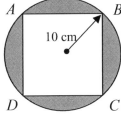

Diagram **NOT**
accurately drawn

Work out the total shaded area.

Give your answer in the form $a\pi + b$, where *a* and *b* are integers.

....

....

....

....

        Answer................................   (4 marks)

8

45

18   Two circles are overlap. *CDE* is an isosceles triangle. *CE* is a tangent to Circle *C2*.

$CD = CE$. $\angle DCE = 2\angle EAB$

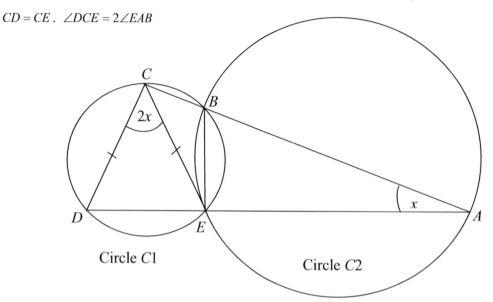

Circle *C1*

Circle *C2*

Prove that *BE* is perpendicular to *AD*.

....

....

....

....

....

....

        Answer…………………………….   (4 marks)

19   The graph shows two lines. $L2$ is a reflection of $L1$: $y = 2 - 2x$ through $y = 2$.

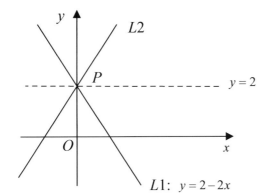

Work out the equation of $L2$.

Give your answer in the form $y = mx + c$.

....

....

....

....

....

....

....

....

....

        Answer................................   (3 marks)

3

20 The graph of $y = x^2 - 5x - 3$ is shown below for values of x between -2 and 7.

By drawing an appropriate straight line, use the graph to solve the equation.

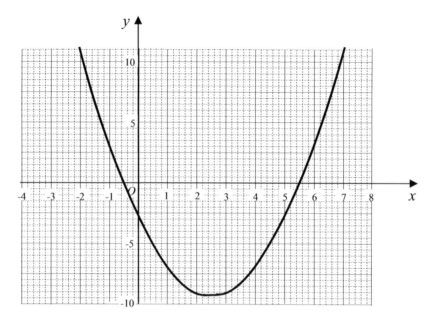

By drawing a suitable linear graph on the grid, work out approximate solutions of $x^2 - 6x - 2 = 0$.

Give your answers to 1 decimal place.

....

....

....

....

....

....

....

....

....

....

....

....

        Answer............................   (5 marks)

Paper 1 solutions

1   The diagram shows a square with side 4 cm. Points *A*, *B*, *C* and *D* are quarter of the ways along the sides.

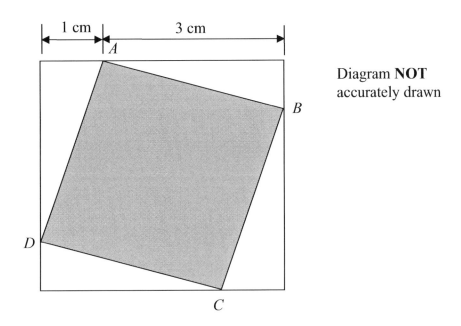

Diagram **NOT** accurately drawn

Work out the proportion of the area inside the square that is shaded.

The area of the 4 right-angled triangles is:

$$\frac{1 \times 3}{2} \times 4 = 6$$

The area of the square with side 4 cm is:

$$4 \times 4 = 16$$

The proportion of the area inside the square, which is shaded, can be calculated as follows:

$$\frac{16 - 6}{16} = \frac{5}{8}$$

Answer $\frac{5}{8}$ (4 marks)

2   Triangle ABC has perimeter 15 cm

$AB = 5$ cm.

$BC = 4$ cm.

Show that ABC is an acute triangle.

$AC = 15 - 5 - 4 = 6$ which is the longest side in the triangle.

$\therefore \angle B$ is the biggest angle in the triangle.

$\cos \angle B = \dfrac{AB^2 + BC^2 - AC^2}{2 \times AB \times BC} = \dfrac{25 + 16 - 36}{2 \times 5 \times 4} = \dfrac{1}{8} > 0 \Rightarrow \angle B < 90^0$

$\therefore ABC$ is an acute triangle.

(4 marks)

3   The diagram shows a solid prism with the same cross-section through its length. The cross-section is a trapezium with height 40 cm. The top $EFGH$ is a rectangle of width 20 cm and length 30 cm, the base $ABCD$ is rectangle of width 20 cm and length 40 cm. The prism is made from wood with density 0.0005 kg/cm³.

Work out the mass of the prism.

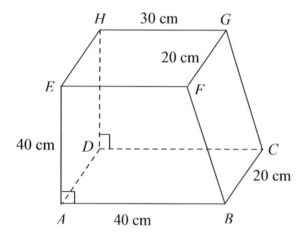

The prism has a height of 20 cm and the cross section with a trapezium.

The volume of the prism is:

$\dfrac{EF + AB}{2} \times AE \times BC$

$\therefore$ The mass of the prism is

$\dfrac{EF + AB}{2} \times AE \times BC \times 0.0005 = \dfrac{30 + 40}{2} \times 40 \times 20 \times 0.0005 = 14$

Answer   14 kg   (4 marks)

8

4   Here are a trapezium and a right-angled triangle. The area of the triangle is the same as the area of the trapezium.

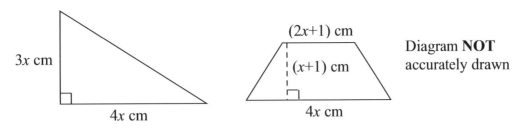

3x cm

(2x+1) cm

(x+1) cm

Diagram **NOT**
accurately drawn

4x cm

4x cm

Show that $6x^2 - 7x = 1$

The area of the triangle is the same as the area of trapezium

$$\frac{3x \times 4x}{2} = \frac{(2x+1+4x)(x+1)}{2} \Rightarrow 12x^2 = 6x^2 + 7x + 1 \Rightarrow 6x^2 - 7x = 1$$

$$\therefore 6x^2 - 7x = 1$$

(4 marks)

5   *BA* is a diameter of this circle and is extended to point *S*. *ST* is a tangent meeting the circle at point *T*. *O* is the centre of the circle. *AT*=*AO*

Prove that triangle *ATB* is congruent to triangle *OTS*.

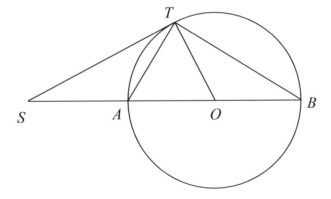

O is the centre of the circle, $\Rightarrow AO = OT$

AT=*AO* $\Rightarrow OT = AT = AO$, $\angle BAT = \angle SOT$

ST is a tangent meeting the circle at point $T \Rightarrow \angle OTS = 90^0$

BA is a diameter of this circle $\Rightarrow \angle ATB = 90^0$

$\Rightarrow \angle OTS = \angle ATB$

$\therefore$ Triangle *ATB* is congruent to triangle *OTS* (ASA)

(4 marks)

8

6   Triangle **A** and triangle **B** are similar.

Triangle **A** has a circumference of 150 cm

Triangle **B** has a circumference of 30 cm

Triangle **A** has an area of 1000 cm²

Calculate the area of triangle **B**.

The area of triangle **B** can be calculated as follows:

$$\frac{\text{Circumference } \textbf{B}}{\text{Circumference } \textbf{A}} = \sqrt{\frac{\text{Area } \textbf{B}}{\text{Area } \textbf{A}}} \Rightarrow \text{Area } \textbf{B} = (\frac{\text{Circumference } \textbf{B}}{\text{Circumference } \textbf{A}})^2 \times \text{Area } \textbf{A}$$

$$\text{Area } \textbf{B} = (\frac{30}{150})^2 \times 1000 = 40$$

Answer   40 cm²   (3 marks)

7   Emma has a biased coin. When the coin is thrown once, the probability that the coin will land heads is 0.4. Emma throws the coin twice.

7(a)   Complete and fully label the probability tree diagram to show the possible outcome.

1st   2nd

(4 marks)

7(b)   Calculate the probability that the coin will land heads at least once.

From the probability tree diagram, the probability the coin lands heads at least once is:

$0.4 \times 0.6 \times 2 + 0.4 \times 0.4 = 0.64$

Alternative method: $1 - 0.6 \times 0.6 = 0.64$ (excluding the probability that the coin lands tails twice)

Answer   0.64   (2 marks)

8   There are 20 boys and 10 girls in a class. They took maths challenge. The mean
     mark for boys is 55%, the mean mark for the class is 50%.

     Work out the mean mark for the girls.

     $$\frac{50\% \times 30 - 55\% \times 20}{10} = 40\%$$

          Answer   40%   (2 marks)

9   The table shows information about the height of some plants.

Height (cm)	$0 < h \le 20$	$20 < h \le 30$	$30 < h \le 40$	$40 < h \le 70$
Number of plants	24	38	33	30

9(a) Complete the histogram for this information.

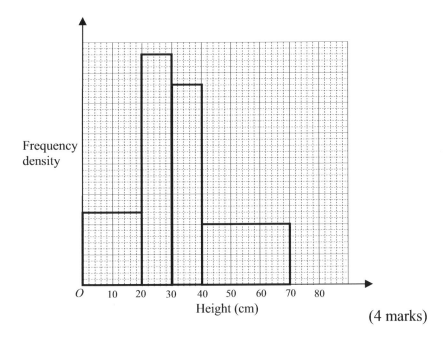

                                                      (4 marks)

9(b) Work out an estimate for the number of plants which the height is greater more than
      52 cm

      $$\frac{30}{15} \times 9 = 18$$

          Answer   18   (3 marks)

10   The first four terms of an arithmetic sequence are

2   6   10   14

Work out an expression, in terms of n, for the nth term.

$a_n = a_1 + (n-1)d$

$d = 6 - 2 = 4$, $a_1 = 2$ where $n = 2$.

$\therefore \quad a_n = 2 + 4(n-1) = 4n - 2$

Answer $4n - 2$ (3 marks)

11(a) Simplify $(p^2 \times p^3)^2$

$(p^2 \times p^3)^2 = (p^{2+3})^2 = (p^5)^2 = p^{5 \times 2} = p^{10}$

Answer p^{10} (2 marks)

11(b) Simplify fully $\dfrac{3x}{(x-2)(x-4)} + \dfrac{3}{x-2}$

$\dfrac{3x}{(x-2)(x-4)} + \dfrac{3}{x-2} = \dfrac{3x}{(x-2)(x-4)} + \dfrac{3(x-4)}{(x-2)(x-4)} = \dfrac{6(x-2)}{(x-2)(x-4)} = \dfrac{6}{x-4}$

Answer $\dfrac{6}{x-4}$ (2 marks)

11(c) Factorise $8x^2 - 18$

$8x^2 - 18 = 2(4x^2 - 9) = 2(2x-3)(2x+3)$

Answer $2(2x-3)(2x+3)$ (2 marks)

12(a) Express $2^{100} + 2^{102}$ in the form $m \times 2^{100}$, m is an integer.

$2^{100} + 2^{102} = 2^{100} + 4 \times 2^{100} = 5 \times 2^{100}$

Answer 5×2^{100} (2 marks)

12(b) Express $2^{100} + 2^{102}$ in the form $n \times 4^{50}$, n is an integer.

$2^{100} + 2^{102} = 4^{50} + 4 \times 4^{50} = 5 \times 4^{50}$

Alternative method: $2^{100} + 2^{102} = 5 \times 2^{100} = 5 \times 2^{2 \times 50} = 5 \times 4^{50}$

Answer 5×4^{50} (2 marks)

13

13(a)   Write 1.5×10^{-4} as an ordinary number.

   Answer   0.00015   (2 marks)

13(b)   Work out the value of $4.8 \times 10^5 \div (4 \times 10^{-6})$

   Give your answer in standard form.

   $4.8 \times 10^5 \div (4 \times 10^{-6}) = \dfrac{4.8}{4} \times 10^{5+6} = 1.2 \times 10^{11}$

   Answer 1.2×10^{11} (2 marks)

14   On 1 April 2019, the cost of 5 grams of gold was £220. The cost of gold increased by 10% from 1 April 2018 to 1 April 2019.

   Work out the cost of 20 grams of gold on 1 April 2018.

   The gold price on 1 April 2019: $\dfrac{£220}{5g} = £44/g$

   The gold price on 1 April 2018: $\dfrac{44}{1+10\%} = £40/g$

   The cost of 20 grams of gold on 1 April 2018: $£40/g \times 20g = £800$

   (Alterative method: $\dfrac{220}{1+10\%} \times 4 = 800$)

   Answer   £800   (3 marks)

15   P is directly proportional to Q^2 where $Q > 0$. $P = 400$ when $Q = 10$.

15(a)   Find a formula for P in terms of Q.

   $P = kQ^2$ where k is a constant.

   $k = \dfrac{P}{Q^2} = \dfrac{400}{10^2} = 4$

   $\therefore P = 4Q^2$

   Answer $P = 4Q^2$ (3 marks)

10

15(b)   Find the value of Q when $P = 36$.

$$P = 4Q^2 \Rightarrow Q = \pm\sqrt{\dfrac{P}{4}}$$

$\because Q > 0$, clearly the negative answer is not suitable here.

$$Q = \sqrt{\dfrac{P}{4}} = \sqrt{\dfrac{36}{4}} = 3$$

Answer   3   (2 marks)

16   a, b, c and d are consecutive integers.

Explain why $ab + cd$ is always even.

$b = a + 1, \quad c = a + 2, \quad d = a + 3$

$ab + cd = a(a+1) + (a+2)(a+3) = a^2 + a + a^2 + 5a + 6 = 2(a^2 + 3a + 3)$

$2(a^2 + 3a + 3)$ is always even

$\therefore \ ab + cd$ is always even.

(3 marks)

17   Solve the simultaneous equations

$2x + y = 13$

$x + y = 8$

$2x + y = 13$ (1)

$x + y = 8$ (2)

Eq. (1)-Eq. (2) $\Rightarrow x = 5 \Rightarrow y = 8 - x = 3$ from Eq. (2)

Answer $x = 5, y = 3$ (2 marks)

18   The diagram shows part of the graph of $y = f(x)$

18(a)   Find $f(3)$

From the graph, $f(3) = 1$

Answer   1   (2 marks)

18(b)   Write down the coordinates of the turning point of the graph

Answer   (2, -1)   (2 marks)

11

56

18(c)   Write down estimates for the roots of $f(x) = 0$.

Give your answers to 1 decimal place.

Answer $x = 1.3$, $x = 2.7$

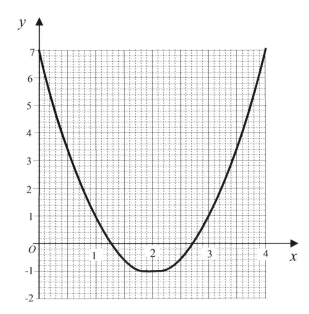

(2 marks)

19   The equation of line L_1 is $y = 2x - 3$

The equation of line L_2 is $2y + x = 10$

Show that these two lines are perpendicular.

The gradient of line L_1 is:

$K_1 = 2$

The gradient of line L_2 is:

$K_2 = -\dfrac{1}{2}$

$K_1 \times K_2 = 2 \times (-\dfrac{1}{2}) = -1$

$\therefore$ These two lines are perpendicular.

(3 marks)

5

20   *OABC* is a parallelogram. *M* is the midpoint of *OC*.

$\overrightarrow{OA} = \mathbf{x}$, $\overrightarrow{AB} = \mathbf{y}$.

Work out the vector of $\overrightarrow{AM}$

Give your answer in terms of **x** and **y**.

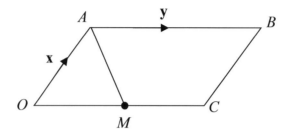

OABC is a parallelogram. *M* is the midpoint of *OC* $\Rightarrow \overrightarrow{OM} = \dfrac{\overrightarrow{AB}}{2} = \dfrac{\mathbf{y}}{2}$

$\overrightarrow{AM} = \overrightarrow{OM} - \overrightarrow{OA} = \dfrac{\mathbf{y}}{2} - \mathbf{x}$

Answer $\overrightarrow{AM} = \dfrac{\mathbf{y}}{2} - \mathbf{x}$ (3 marks)

3

Paper 2 solutions

1(a) Expand and simplify $(3+2\sqrt{3})(2+3\sqrt{3})$

Give your answer in the form $a+b\sqrt{3}$, where a and b are integers.

Show your working clearly.

$(3+2\sqrt{3})(2+3\sqrt{3}) = 6+9\sqrt{3}+4\sqrt{3}+6(\sqrt{3})^2 = 24+13\sqrt{3}$

Answer $24+13\sqrt{3}$ (2 marks)

1(b) Factorise $16x^2-9$

$16x^2-9 = (4x)^2-9 = (4x-3)(4x+3)$

Answer $(4x-3)(4x+3)$ (2 marks)

1(c) Simplify the expression $(2x^3y^2)^3$

$(2x^3y^2)^3 = 2^3 x^{3\times3} y^{2\times3} = 8x^9y^6$

Answer $8x^9y^6$ (2 marks)

2 Solve the equation $x^2-4x-2=0$

Give your answer in the form $a\pm\sqrt{b}$, where a and b are integers.

$x = \dfrac{4\pm\sqrt{16+4\times2}}{2} = 2\pm\sqrt{6}$

Answer $2\pm\sqrt{6}$ (2 marks)

3 Rationalise the denominator and simply fully $\dfrac{6}{\sqrt{3}-3}$

$\dfrac{6}{\sqrt{3}-3} = \dfrac{6(\sqrt{3}+3)}{3-9} = -\sqrt{3}-3$

Answer $-\sqrt{3}-3$ (2 marks)

4 Work out the range of values of x for which $x^2-3x-10<0$

$x^2-3x-10<0 \Rightarrow (x+2)(x-5)>0 \Rightarrow -2<x<5$

Answer $-2<x<5$ (2 marks)

12

59

5   Find an approximate value for $\dfrac{4.125\times10^6}{7.997\times10^{-4}}$

Give your answer in standard form.

$$\frac{4.125\times10^6}{7.997\times10^{-4}} \approx \frac{4\times10^6}{8\times10^{-4}} = 0.5\times10^{10} = 5\times10^9$$

Answer 5×10^9 (3 marks)

6   A bag contains red and blue beads. The ratio of red beads to blue beads is 3:2.

The number of red beads is decreased by 20%.

The number of blue beads is increased by 40%

There are now 52 beads in total in the bag.

Work out how many blue beads were originally.

If the number of blue beads originally was x, the number of red beads originally was $\dfrac{3}{2}x$.

$$\frac{3}{2}x(1-20\%)+x(1+40\%)=52 \Rightarrow x=20$$

Answer   20   (3 marks)

7   A line passes through $(4,3)$ with gradient 2.

Work out the equation of the line and write down the equation in the form $y=mx+c$

$$y-3=2(x-4) \Rightarrow y=2x-5$$

Answer $y=2x-5$ (2 marks)

8    $(m+p)x+(m-p) \equiv 4x+6$, where m and p are integers.

Work out the values of m and p.

$m+p=4$ (1)

$m-p=6$ (2)

Eq. (1)+Eq. (2)$\Rightarrow 2m=10 \Rightarrow m=5$, $p=4-m=-1$ from Eq. (1).

Answer $m=5$, $p=-1$ (2 marks)

10

9   You are given that $5.6 \times 13.2 = 73.92$ exactly.

9(a)   Emma says that $56 \times 0.0132 = 7.392$

Without doing an exact calculation, show that Emma is wrong.

$$\frac{56}{5.6} = 10, \quad \frac{0.0132}{13.2} = 0.001$$

$$56 \times 0.0132 = 73.92 \times 10 \times 0.001 = 73.92 \times 0.01 = 0.7392$$

(3 marks)

9(b)   Find the exact value of 0.056×132

$$0.056 \times 132 = 0.01 \times 10 \times 73.92 = 7.392$$

         Answer   7.392   (3 marks)

10   P is inversely proportional to Q^2 where $Q > 0$. $P = 100$ when $Q = 6$.

Find the value of Q when $P = 36$.

$$P = \frac{k}{Q^2} \Rightarrow 100 = \frac{k}{6^2} \Rightarrow k = 3600$$

$$\because Q > 0, \ Q = \sqrt{\frac{k}{P}} = \sqrt{\frac{3600}{36}} = 10$$

         Answer   10   (3 marks)

9

11   *PQRS* is a trapezium, as shown in the diagram. $\angle SPQ = 60^0$. *RQ* is perpendicular to *SR* and *PQ*.

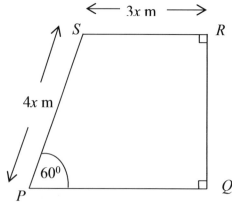

Work out the area of the trapezium, in terms of *x*

The area of the trapezium is

$$\frac{(SR + PQ) \times SP \times \sin 60^0}{2} = \frac{(SR + SR + SP \times \cos 60^0) \times SP \times \sin 60^0}{2}$$

$$= \frac{(3x + 3x + 4x \times \frac{1}{2}) \times 4x \times \frac{\sqrt{3}}{2}}{2} = 8\sqrt{3}x^2$$

Answer $8\sqrt{3}x^2$ m^2 (3 marks)

12   Here is a triangle. $\sin x^0 = \frac{3\sqrt{3}}{8}$

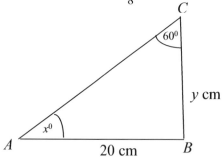

Work out the value of *y*.

$$\frac{BC}{\sin A} = \frac{AB}{\sin C} \Rightarrow \frac{y}{\sin x^0} = \frac{20}{\sin 60^0} \Rightarrow y = \frac{20 \times \sin x^0}{\sin 60^0} = \frac{20 \times \frac{3\sqrt{3}}{8}}{\frac{\sqrt{3}}{2}} = 15$$

Answer   15   (3 marks)

6

13   *A, B, C* and *D* are on the circumference of a circle, *DT* is a tangent to the circle at *D*.

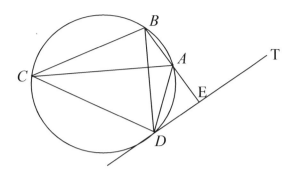

Prove that triangle *ADE* is similar to triangle *DBE*.

DT is a tangent to the circle at $D \Rightarrow \angle ADE = \angle DBE$

$\angle AED = \angle BED$

∴ Triangle *ADE* is similar to triangle *DBE* (AA)

(3 marks)

14   *OABC* is a parallelogram. *M* is the midpoint of *OC*.

$\overrightarrow{OA} = \mathbf{x}$, $\overrightarrow{AB} = \mathbf{y}$.

Show by a vector method that *AM* is parallel to *OD*

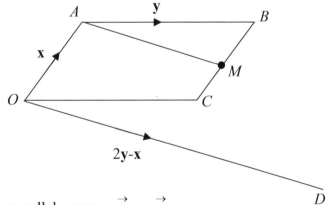

OABC is a parallelogram $\Rightarrow \overrightarrow{CB} = \overrightarrow{OA} = x$

M is the midpoint of $OC \Rightarrow \overrightarrow{MB} = \dfrac{x}{2}$

$\overrightarrow{AM} = \overrightarrow{AB} + \overrightarrow{BM} = \overrightarrow{AB} - \overrightarrow{MB} = y - \dfrac{x}{2}$

$\overrightarrow{OD} = 2y - x = 2\,\overrightarrow{AM}$

∴ *AM* is parallel to *OD*

(3 marks)

6

15(a)   Shape **P** is reflected in the *x*-axis to give shape **Q**.

Shape **Q** is reflected in the line *x* = -1 to give shape **R**.

Describe fully the single transformation that maps shape **P** onto shape **R**

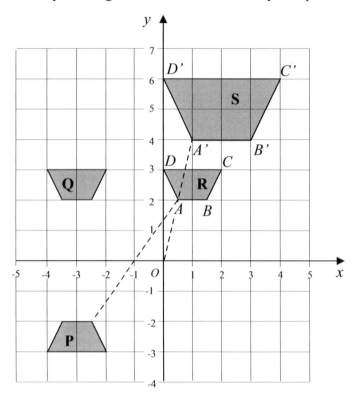

Answer   Rotation 180⁰ about (-1,0)   (3 marks)

15(b)   On the grid, enlarge shape **R** with scale factor 2 and centre *O*, and label it **S** on the grid.

To enlarge shape **R** with scale factor 2 and centre *O* to get shape **S**,

extend *OA* to *A'* so that *OA'* is twice *OA* to get the vertex *A'* of shape **S**.

In the same way, get the other vertexes, *B'*, *C'* and *D'* of shape **S**.

(3 marks)

16   A box contains toy cars. Each car is red or black or blue.

Jack takes a car at random from the box.

The table shows the probabilities that Jack takes a red car or a blue car.

Colour of car	Probability
red	0.50
blue	0.30
black	

16(a)   Work out the probability that Jack takes a black car.

The probability that Jack takes a black car is:

$1 - 0.50 - 0.30 = 0.20$

Answer   0.20   (2 marks)

16(b)   Jack adds 50 black cars into the box. The following table shows the probabilities that Jack takes a red car or a blue car or a black car or silver after he adds 50 black cars into the box.

Colour of car	Probability
red	0.40
blue	0.24
black	0.36

Work out the total number of cars in the box originally.

The total number of cars in the box originally is x

$0.36(x + 50) - 0.20x = 50 \Rightarrow x = 200$

Answer   200   (4 marks)

17   The scatter graph shows the heights of boys at different ages.

17(a) Draw a line of best fit on the scatter graph.

A line of best fit on the scatter graph is shown below

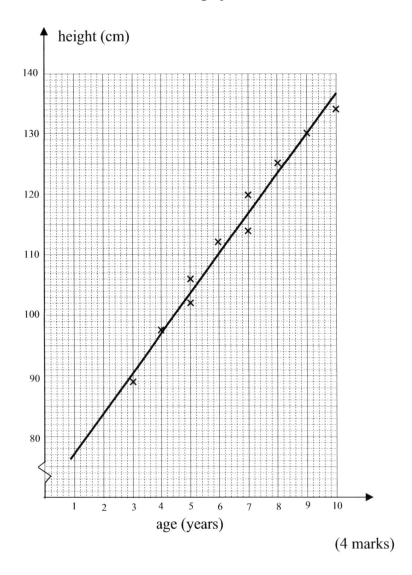

age (years)

(4 marks)

17(b) Estimate the height of a one year old and comment on the reliability of your estimate.

Answer   the height of a one year old is 74 cm

Possibly not reliable as it outside the range covered by the line of best fit.

(3 marks)

18   100 pupils took an examination paper. The table gives a summary of their results.

	Marks
Minimum	17
Lower quartile	46
Median	58
Upper quartile	72
Maximum	92

18(a)   Draw a box plot to represent this information.

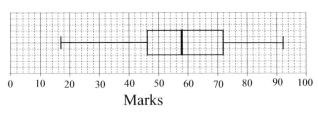

Marks

(3 marks)

18(b)   Write down the interquartile range for these data.

The interquartile range is:

Upper quartile – Lower quartile = 72 – 46 =26

Answer   26   (2 marks)

18(c)   Work out an estimate for the number of these pupils with marks between 17 and 72.

17 marks are minimum.

72 marks are upper quartile.

The number of these pupils with marks between 17 and 72 can be estimated by $\frac{3}{4}$

of the pupils.

$\frac{3}{4} \times 100 = 75$

Answer   75   (2 marks)

18(d)   Draw a cumulative frequency diagram to show the information.

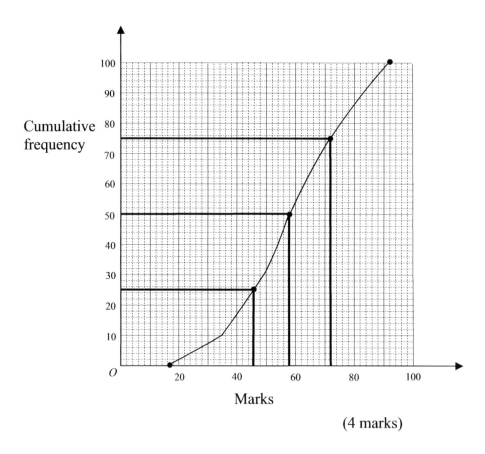

(4 marks)

19   The diagram shows a circle, centre *C*. *TP* is a tangent to the circle and intersects the circle at *P*.

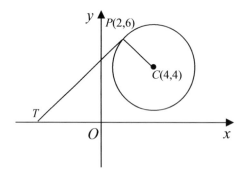

Work out the equation of line *TP*.

TP is a tangent to the circle, $\therefore$ *TP* is perpendicular to *CP*

The gradient of *CP* is $\dfrac{6-4}{2-4} = -1$, the gradient of *TP* is 1.

The equation of line *TP* passing through (2,6) wih gradient 1 is:

$y - 6 = x - 2 \Rightarrow y = x + 4$

Answer $y = x + 4$ (3 marks)

7

20   Here is the graph of $y = -2(x-2)^2 + 2$ for values of x from 0 to 4.

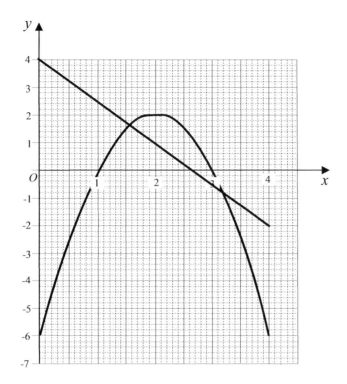

By drawing a suitable linear graph on the grid, work out approximate solutions of

$4x^2 - 19x + 20 = 0$.

Give your answers to 1 decimal place.

$y = -2(x-2)^2 + 2$ (1)

$4x^2 - 19x + 20 = 0$ (2)

$2 \times$ Eq. (1) - Eq. (2) $\Rightarrow y = -\dfrac{3}{2}x + 4$

Draw the line $y = -\dfrac{3}{2}x + 4$ on the graph $\Rightarrow x = 1.6$ or $x = 3.2$

Answer   1.6 , 3.2   (4 marks)

4

Paper 3 solutions

1   Factorise fully $(x^2-16)+(x+4)(x+2)$

$(x^2-16)+(x+4)(x+2)$
$=(x+4)(x-4)+(x+4)(x+2)$
$=(x+4)(x-4+x+2)$
$=(x+4)(2x-2)$
$=2(x+4)(x-1)$

        Answer $2(x+4)(x-1)$ **(2 marks)**

2      $x^2+px+q\equiv(x+2)^2+3$

Work out the values of p and q.

$$x^2+px+q=(x+\frac{p}{2})^2-(\frac{p}{2})^2+q$$

$$\therefore \frac{p}{2}=2\Rightarrow p=4,\quad -(\frac{p}{2})^2+q=3\Rightarrow q=3+(\frac{p}{2})^2=3+4=7$$

        Answer $p=4,\quad q=7$ **(2 marks)**

(Alternative method: $(x+2)^2+3=x^2+4x+7$, $\therefore p=4,\quad q=7$)

3   Simplify $(p^2\times p^3)^2$

$(p^2\times p^3)^2=(p^{2+3})^2=p^{5\times 2}=p^{10}$

        Answer p^{10} **(2 marks)**

4   Simplify fully $\dfrac{x+22}{(x-2)(x+4)}+\dfrac{3}{x+4}$

$$\frac{x+22}{(x-2)(x+4)}+\frac{3}{x+4}=\frac{x+22}{(x-2)(x+4)}+\frac{3(x-2)}{(x-2)(x+4)}=\frac{4x+16}{(x-2)(x+4)}=\frac{4(x+4)}{(x-2)(x+4)}=\frac{4}{x-2}$$

        Answer $\dfrac{4}{x-2}$ **(2 marks)**

5(a)   Solve $(6-\sqrt{x})^{\frac{1}{2}}=2$

$$(6-\sqrt{x})^{\frac{1}{2}}=2\Rightarrow 6-\sqrt{x}=4\Rightarrow \sqrt{x}=2\Rightarrow x=4$$

        Answer   4   **(2 marks)**

5(b) Solve $x^3 - 4x = 0$

$x^3 - 4x = 0 \Rightarrow x(x-2)(x+2) = 0 \Rightarrow x = 0,\ x = 2 \text{ or } x = -2$

   Answer   -2, 0, 2,   (3 marks)

6      $x : y = 5 : 3$ and $a : b = 5x : 3y$

Work out $a : b$

Give your answer in its simplest form.

$$\frac{a}{b} = \frac{5x}{3y} = \frac{5}{3} \times \frac{x}{y} = \frac{5}{3} \times \frac{5}{3} = \frac{25}{9}$$

   Answer $25 : 9$ (2 marks)

7   Express 72 as the products of its prime factors.

$72 = 2 \times 2 \times 2 \times 3 \times 3$

   Answer $2 \times 2 \times 2 \times 3 \times 3$ (2 marks)

8   Work out 104×96

$104 \times 96 = (100 + 4)(100 - 4) = 100^2 - 4^2 = 10000 - 16 = 9984$

   Answer   9984   (2 marks)

9(a)   Work out $4\frac{2}{7} + 1\frac{2}{3}$

$$4\frac{2}{7} + 1\frac{2}{3} = 4\frac{6}{21} + 1\frac{14}{21} = 5\frac{20}{21}$$

   Answer $5\frac{20}{21}$ (3 marks)

9(b)   Work out $4\frac{2}{7} \div 1\frac{2}{3}$

Give your answer as a mixed number in its simplest form.

$$4\frac{2}{7} \div 1\frac{2}{3} = \frac{30}{7} \div \frac{5}{3} = \frac{\overset{6}{\cancel{30}}}{7} \times \frac{3}{\underset{1}{\cancel{5}}} = \frac{18}{7} = 2\frac{4}{7}$$

   Answer $2\frac{4}{7}$ (3 marks)

15

10   Expand and simplify $(x-1)(x-2)(x+2)$

$(x-1)(x-2)(x+2) = (x-1)(x^2-4) = x^3 - x^2 - 4x + 4$

Answer $x^3 - x^2 - 4x + 4$ (3 marks)

11   Emma buys a jumper.

20% VAT is added to the price of the jumper.

Emma has to pay a total of £60.

What is the price of the jumper with **no** VAT added?

$x(1+20\%) = 60 \Rightarrow x = 50$

Answer   £50   (3 marks)

12   In triangle ABC, $\cos B = \dfrac{1}{3}$

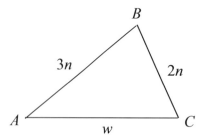

Show that triangle ABC is isosceles.

$AC^2 = w^2 = (2n)^2 + (3n)^2 - 2 \times 2n \times 3n \times \cos B = 4n^2 + 9n^2 - 12n^2 \times \dfrac{1}{3} = 9n^2 = AB^2$

$\therefore$ Triangle ABC is isosceles.

(5 marks)

13   Here are a sphere and a cone. The base of the cone and the sphere have the same radius r cm. l, the slant height, is $\sqrt{17}r$ cm.

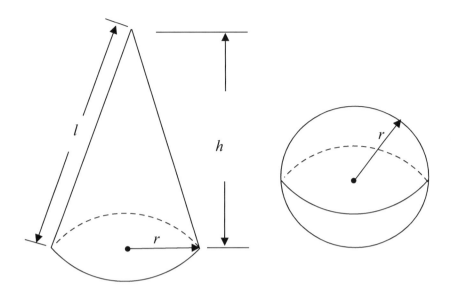

Prove that the sphere and the cone have the same volume.

h is the height of the cone.

$$l = \sqrt{h^2 + r^2} \Rightarrow h = \sqrt{l^2 - r^2} = \sqrt{17r^2 - r^2} = 4r$$

The volume of the sphere is $\dfrac{4}{3}\pi r^3$

The volume of the cone is $\dfrac{1}{3}\pi r^2 h = \dfrac{1}{3}\pi r^2 \times 4r = \dfrac{4}{3}\pi r^3$

$\therefore$ The sphere and the cone have the same volume.

(5 marks)

5

14   Point P and vectors **a** and **b** are shown on the grid.

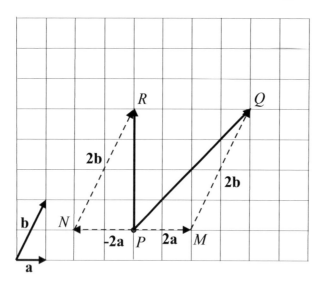

14(a) $\overrightarrow{PQ} = 2\mathbf{a} + 2\mathbf{b}$

On the grid, mark vector $\overrightarrow{PQ}$

Firstly from P, draw 2**a**, $\overrightarrow{PM} = 2\mathbf{a}$,

Secondly from M, draw 2**b**, $\overrightarrow{MQ} = 2\mathbf{b}$,

$\therefore \overrightarrow{PQ} = \overrightarrow{PM} + \overrightarrow{MQ} = 2\mathbf{a} + 2\mathbf{b}$

$\overrightarrow{PQ}$ is as shown on the diagram.   (5 marks)

14(b) $\overrightarrow{PR} = -2\mathbf{a} + 2\mathbf{b}$

On the grid, mark vector $\overrightarrow{PR}$

In the same method as part (a) above, draw $\overrightarrow{PN} = -2\mathbf{a}$, $\overrightarrow{NR} = 2\mathbf{b}$.

$\therefore \overrightarrow{PR} = -2\mathbf{a} + 2\mathbf{b}$

$\overrightarrow{PR}$ is as shown on the diagram.   (5 marks)

10

15   Find an equation of the line that is parallel to the line $y = 3x - 2$ and passes through the point (3,5).

$y - 5 = 3(x - 3) \Rightarrow y = 3x - 4$

Answer $y = 3x - 4$ (3 marks)

16   The diagram shows the graph of $y = \sin x$ for $0^0 \leq x \leq 360^0$

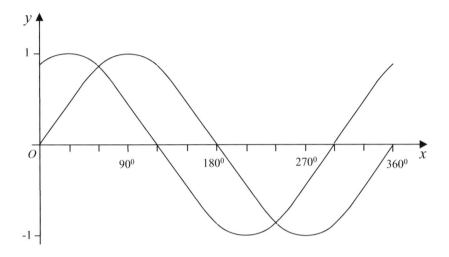

On the diagram above, sketch the graph of $y = \sin(x + 60^0)$ for $0^0 \leq x \leq 360^0$

As shown on the graph.

(4 marks)

7

17   Here is the graph of $y = 2(x-2)^2 - 1$ for values of x from 0 to 4.

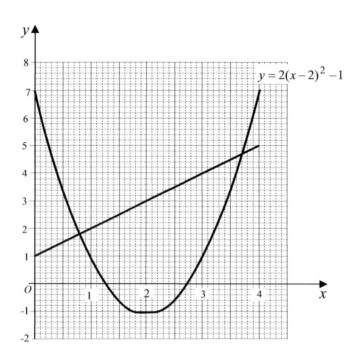

By drawing a suitable linear graph on the grid, work out approximate solutions of

$2x^2 - 9x + 6 = 0$.

Give your answers to 1 decimal place.

$y = 2(x-2)^2 - 1$ (1)

$2x^2 - 9x + 6 = 0$ (2)

Eq. (1) + Eq. (2) $\Rightarrow y = x + 1$

Draw the line $y = x + 1$ on the graph $\Rightarrow x = 0.8$ or $x = 3.7$

            Answer   0.8 , 3.7   (4 marks)

18   Mr Smith gives his class a test.

        10 girls in the class get a mean mark of 66%

        20 boys in the class get a mean mark of 72%

        Work out the mean mark for the whole class.

        $\dfrac{10 \times 66\% + 20 \times 72\%}{30} = 70\%$

            Answer   70%   (3 marks)

7

76

19   Emma keeps a record of the time that the school bus takes her from her home to school. Her record for last month is shown in the table.

Time, t minutes	Frequency
$10 < t \leq 12$	5
$12 < t \leq 14$	10
$14 < t \leq 16$	4
$16 < t \leq 18$	1

19(a)   There are 200 school days in the year.

Use the information in the table to estimate the number of days in a year on which Emma's bus journey takes more than 14 minutes. (Emma never misses a day of school.)

The record shows that there are 5 days which Emma's bus journey takes more than 14 minutes in the period of 20 days.

∴ The number of days in a year on which Emma's bus journey takes more than 14 minutes is:

$\dfrac{200}{20} \times 5 = 50$

Answer   50 days   (4 marks)

19(b)   What is the probability that, on a randomly chosen day, the journey takes less than 12 minutes?

The record shows that there are 5 days which Emma's bus journey takes less than 12 minutes in the period of 20 days.

The probability, which the journey takes less than 12 minutes, is:

$\dfrac{5}{20} = 0.25$

Answer   0.25   (4 marks)

8

20   A box contains toy cars. Each car is red or black or blue.

Jack takes a car at random from the box.

The table shows the probabilities that Jack takes a red car or a blue car.

Colour of car	Probability
red	0.50
blue	0.30
black	

20(a)   Work out the probability that Jack takes a black car.

The probability that Jack takes a black car is:

$1 - 0.50 - 0.30 = 0.20$

Answer   0.20   (3 marks)

20(b)   Jack puts the car back into the box. There are 4 black cars in the box.

Work out the number of red cars and the number of blue cars in the box.

Colour of car	The number of cars
red	
blue	

The number of red cars is 2.5 times black cars.

The number of blue cars is 1.5 times black cars.

$\therefore$ The number of red cars is: $2.5 \times 4 = 10$

The number of blue cars is: $1.5 \times 4 = 6$

(4 marks)

Paper 4 solutions

1(a) a is a positive integer, show that $\sqrt{3a}(\sqrt{27a}+a\sqrt{3a})$ is always a multiple of 3.

$$\sqrt{3a}(\sqrt{27a}+a\sqrt{3a})=\sqrt{3a}(3\sqrt{3a}+a\sqrt{3a})=9a+3a^2=3(3a+a^2)$$

$$\therefore \sqrt{3a}(\sqrt{27a}+a\sqrt{3a}) \text{ is always a multiple of 3}$$

(2 marks)

1(b) By factorising fully, simplify $\dfrac{x^4-3x^3+2x^2}{x^4-5x^2+4}$

$$\frac{x^4-3x^3+2x^2}{x^4-5x^2+4}=\frac{x^2(x^2-3x+2)}{(x^2-1)(x^2-4)}=\frac{x^2(x-1)(x-2)}{(x-1)(x+1)(x-2)(x+2)}=\frac{x^2}{(x+1)(x+2)}$$

Answer $\dfrac{x^2}{(x+1)(x+2)}$ (2 marks)

2   Rearrange $\dfrac{1}{x}+\dfrac{1}{y}=\dfrac{1}{w}$ to make y the subject.

$$\frac{1}{x}+\frac{1}{y}=\frac{1}{w}\Rightarrow\frac{1}{y}=\frac{x-w}{xw}\Rightarrow y=\frac{xw}{x-w}$$

Answer $y=\dfrac{xw}{x-w}$ (2 marks)

3(a) Find the lowest common multiple (LCM) of 8, 12 and 15

$8=2\times2\times2$, $12=2\times2\times3$, $15=3\times5$

$\therefore$ LCM $=2\times2\times2\times3\times5=120$

Answer   120   (3 marks)

3(b) Find the highest common factor (HCF) of 12, 18 and 36

$12=2\times2\times3$, $18=2\times3\times3$, $36=2\times2\times3\times3$

$\therefore$ HCF $=2\times3=6$

Answer   6   (2 marks)

4(a) Solve $(2-\sqrt{x})^{\frac{1}{3}}=-1$

$$(2-\sqrt{x})^{\frac{1}{3}}=-1\Rightarrow 2-\sqrt{x}=-1\Rightarrow\sqrt{x}=3\Rightarrow x=9$$

Answer   9   (3 marks)

14

4(b)   Solve $\sqrt{12} + \sqrt{48} = \sqrt{27} + \sqrt{x}$

$\sqrt{12} + \sqrt{48} = \sqrt{27} + \sqrt{x} \Rightarrow 2\sqrt{3} + 4\sqrt{3} = 3\sqrt{3} + \sqrt{x} \Rightarrow \sqrt{x} = 3\sqrt{3} \Rightarrow x = 27$

Answer   27   (3 marks)

4(c)   Solve the simultaneous equations

$x^2 + y^2 = 10$ and $y = x + 4$

You must show your working.

Substitute $y = x + 4$ (1)

$x^2 + x^2 + 8x + 16 = 10 \Rightarrow x^2 + 4x + 3 = 0 \Rightarrow (x+3)(x+1) = 0 \Rightarrow x = -1$ or $x = -3$

When $x = -1$, $y = 3$ from Eq. (1); when $x = -3$, $y = 1$ from Eq. (1).

$\therefore$ $x = -1$, $y = 3$ or $x = -3$, $y = 1$

          Answer $x = -1, y = 3$ or $x = -3, y = 1$ (2 marks)

5(a)   Work out $3\frac{1}{3} \div 1\frac{3}{7}$

Give your answer as a mixed number in its simplest form.

$$3\frac{1}{3} \div 1\frac{3}{7} = \frac{\overset{1}{\cancel{10}}}{3} \times \frac{7}{\underset{1}{\cancel{10}}} = \frac{7}{3} = 2\frac{1}{3}$$

          Answer $2\frac{1}{3}$ (3 marks)

5(b)   Rationalise the denominator and simply fully $\dfrac{\sqrt{2} - 1}{2 - \sqrt{2}}$

$$\frac{\sqrt{2}-1}{2-\sqrt{2}} = \frac{(\sqrt{2}-1)(2+\sqrt{2})}{(2-\sqrt{2})(2+\sqrt{2})} = \frac{2\sqrt{2}+2-\sqrt{2}-2}{2} = \frac{\sqrt{2}}{2}$$

          Answer $\dfrac{\sqrt{2}}{2}$ (3 marks)

6   Write $2x^2 - 12x + 5$ in the form $a(x+b)^2 + c$, where a, b and c are integers.

$2x^2 - 12x + 5 = 2(x^2 - 6x + 3^2) - 2 \times 3^2 + 5 = 2(x-3)^2 - 13$

          Answer $2(x-3)^2 - 13$ (3 marks)

14

7   Use ruler and compasses to construct the bisector of angle *ABC*.

You must show all your construction lines.

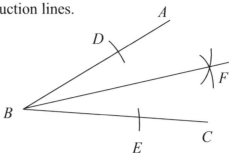

Firstly draw arcs with the same radius and centre *B*, intersect line *AB* at *D* and intersect line *BC* at *E*.

Secondly draw arcs with centres *D* and *E*, with the same radius, respectively. The two arcs meet at *F*.

Draw line *BF*, line *BF* is the bisector of angle *ABC*.

(2 marks)

8   Find an approximate value for $8.96 \div 0.295$

You must show all your working.

$8.96 \div 0.295 \approx 9 \div 3 = 3$

Answer   3   (3 marks)

9   Write $0.\dot{3}\dot{6}$ as a fraction in its simplest form.

$x = 0.\dot{3}\dot{6}$ (1)

$100x = 36.\dot{3}\dot{6}$ (2)

Eq. (2)-Eq. (1) $\Rightarrow 99x = 36 \Rightarrow x = \dfrac{36}{99} = \dfrac{4}{11}$

Answer $\dfrac{4}{11}$ (3 marks)

10   The lengths of the sides of a triangle are in the ratios 2 : 4 : 5. The length of the longest side of the triangle is 30 cm.

Work out the perimeter of the triangle.

If the perimeter of the triangle is *x*, then $x \times \dfrac{5}{11} = 30 \Rightarrow x = \dfrac{30}{5} \times 11 = 66$

Answer   66 cm   (4 marks)

12

11 Jack buys 10 kg of sweets to sell. He pays £10 for the sweets. Jack puts all the sweets into bags. He puts 250 g of sweets into each bag. He sells each bag of sweets for 45p. Jack sells all the bags of sweets.

Work out his percentage profit.

The number of bags for the 10 kg of sweets is: $\dfrac{10000}{250} = 40$

The profit is: $40 \times £0.45 - £10 = £8$

His percentage profit is: $\dfrac{£8}{£10} = 80\%$

Answer   80%   (4 marks)

12 There are 6 blue marbles and 4 red marbles in a bag. Two marbles are taken at random from the bag.

Calculate, as an exactly fraction, the probability that both marbles are the same colour.

The probability, when both are red marbles, is: $\dfrac{4}{10} \times \dfrac{3}{9}$

The probability, when both are blue marbles, is: $\dfrac{6}{10} \times \dfrac{5}{9}$

∴ The probability that both marbles are the same colour is: $\dfrac{4}{10} \times \dfrac{3}{9} + \dfrac{6}{10} \times \dfrac{5}{9} = \dfrac{7}{15}$

Answer $\dfrac{7}{15}$ (4 marks)

13 Chocolate Bars are sold in two sizes.

A standard bar costs 50p and weighs 100 g. A king-size bar costs £1.00 and weighs 250 g.

Which size of bar is the better value for money?

The standard bar price: $\dfrac{50p}{100g} = 0.5p/g$

The king-size bar price: $\dfrac{100p}{250g} = 0.4p/g$

∴ The king-size bar is the better value for money.

Answer   king-size bar   (4 marks)

12

14   A company produces mugs in two sizes.

Small mugs are 6 cm high and can hold 100 cm³ of liquid.

Large mugs are 12 cm high and are identical in shape to small mugs.

Work out the volume of a large mug.

$$\frac{\text{volume of large mug}}{\text{volume of small mug}} = (\frac{\text{height of large mug}}{\text{height of small mug}})^3$$

$$\text{volume of large mug} = (\frac{\text{height of large mug}}{\text{height of small mug}})^3 \times \text{volume of small mug} = (\frac{12}{6})^3 \times 100 = 800$$

Answer   800 cm³   (4 marks)

15   The diagram below shows a solid.

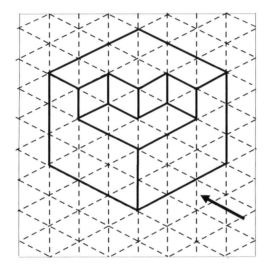

On the grid below, draw the elevation of this solid as seen from the direction of the arrow.   (4 marks)

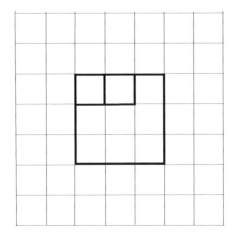

16   *ABC* and *DEA* are straight lines. *BE* is parallel to *CD*. $\angle DAC = 45^0$, $\angle ACD = 50^0$

Work out the size of $\angle AEB$.

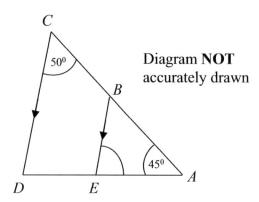

Diagram **NOT** accurately drawn

BE is parallel to $CD \Rightarrow \angle AEB = \angle ADC$

In triangle *ADC*, $\angle ADC = 180^0 - \angle DAC - \angle ACD = 180^0 - 45^0 - 50^0 = 85^0$

$\therefore \ \angle AEB = 85^0$

Answer 85^0 (4 marks)

17   A circle touches all vertices of the square. The radius of the circle is 10 cm as shown.

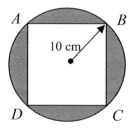

Diagram **NOT** accurately drawn

Work out the total shaded area.

Give your answer in the form $a\pi + b$, where *a* and *b* are integers.

The total shaded area $= \pi r^2 - (\sqrt{2}r)^2 = \pi r^2 - 2r^2 = 100\pi - 200$

Answer $(100\pi - 200) \text{ cm}^2$ (4 marks)

18   Two circles are overlap. *CDE* is an isosceles triangle. *CE* is a tangent to Circle *C2*.

$CD = CE$. $\angle DCE = 2\angle EAB$

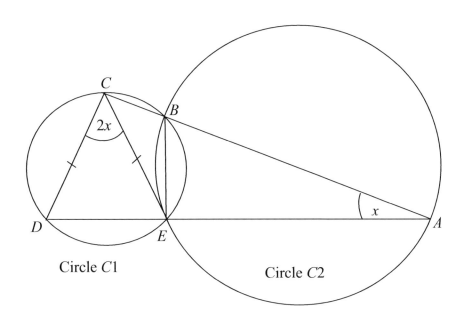

Circle *C1*

Circle *C2*

Prove that *BE* is perpendicular to *AD*.

CE is a tangent to Circle *C2*, $\therefore\ \angle CEB = x$

$CD = CE$, $\therefore\ \angle CED = \dfrac{180^0 - 2x}{2} = 90^0 - x$, $\angle CEB + \angle CED = 90^0$

$\therefore\ \angle AEB = 180^0 - (\angle CEB + \angle CED) = 180^0 - 90^0 = 90^0$

$\therefore$ *BE* is perpendicular to *AD*

(4 marks)

4

19   The graph shows two lines. *L2* is a reflection of *L1*: $y = 2 - 2x$ through $y = 2$.

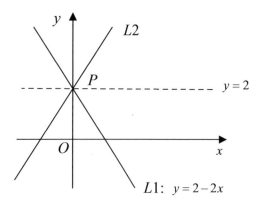

Work out the equation of *L2*.

Give your answer in the form $y = mx + c$.

L1: $y = 2 - 2x \Rightarrow P(0,2)$.

L2 passes through points *P* with gradient 2.

The equation of *L2* is:

$y - 2 = 2(x - 0) \Rightarrow y = 2x + 2$

Answer $y = 2x + 2$ (3 marks)

3

20   The graph of $y = x^2 - 5x - 3$ is shown below for values of x between -2 and 7.

By drawing an appropriate straight line, use the graph to solve the equation.

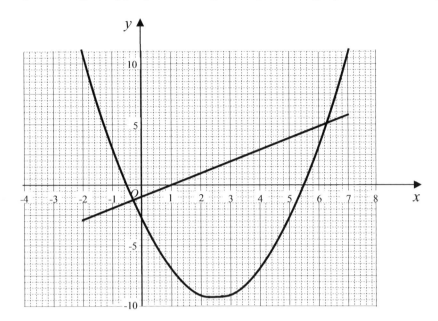

By drawing a suitable linear graph on the grid, work out approximate solutions of

$x^2 - 6x - 2 = 0$.

Give your answers to 1 decimal place.

$y = x^2 - 5x - 3$ (1)

$x^2 - 6x - 2 = 0$ (2)

Eq. (1) + Eq. (2) $\Rightarrow y = x - 1$

Draw the line $y = x - 1$ on the graph $\Rightarrow x = -0.3$ or $x = 6.3$

Answer -0.3 , 6.3 (5 marks)

5

Printed in Poland
by Amazon Fulfillment
Poland Sp. z o.o., Wrocław

53794983R00051